T0193112

Adventure Box Devotions

Outdoor Adventure Devotions for Families

Stephanie Paddock

WESTBOW
PRESS®
A DIVISION OF THOMAS NELSON
& ZONDERVAN

This book is a work of non-fiction. Unless otherwise noted, the author and the publisher make no explicit guarantees as to the accuracy of the information contained in this book and in some cases, names of people and places have been altered to protect their privacy.

WestBow Press books may be ordered through booksellers or by contacting:

WestBow Press
A Division of Thomas Nelson & Zondervan
1663 Liberty Drive
Bloomington, IN 47403
www.westbowpress.com
844-714-3454

Because of the dynamic nature of the Internet, any web addresses or links contained in this book may have changed since publication and may no longer be valid. The views expressed in this work are solely those of the author and do not necessarily reflect the views of the publisher, and the publisher hereby disclaims any responsibility for them.

Any people depicted in stock imagery provided by Getty Images are models, and such images are being used for illustrative purposes only. Certain stock imagery © Getty Images.

Scripture quotations marked (NLT) are taken from the Holy Bible, New Living Translation, copyright ©1996, 2004, 2015 by Tyndale House Foundation. Used by permission of Tyndale House Publishers, a Division of Tyndale House Ministries, Carol Stream, Illinois 60188. All rights reserved.

Interior Image Credit: Cassidy Buchanan

ISBN: 978-1-6642-3249-5 (sc)
ISBN: 978-1-6642-3250-1 (e)

Library of Congress Control Number: 2021909234

Print information available on the last page.

WestBow Press rev. date: 06/08/2021

Wherever you go,
whatever you do,
whatever you see,
may you experience
Jesus in the midst
of your adventures.

Stephanie Paddock

"Direct your children onto the right path, and
when they are older, they will not leave it."

Proverbs 22:6

TABLE OF CONTENTS

5   Introduction

7   How To Use This Devotional

8   Grab Your Gear

ADVENTURES:

9   On a Path – *God helps us make right decisions that lead us to life.*

12   By a Stream – *We need to set aside time to rest with Jesus.*

15   Sitting Around a Campfire – *Jesus is closer than you think!*

18   Goin' Fishin' – *Jesus has something better for us.*

21   On a Highway – *How can you be a blessing to those around you?*

24   Walking Among the Wildflowers – *Jesus is the security we need.*

27   Entering a Cave – *God is with us when we are hurt and afraid.*

30   Stargazing – *You have special abilities to make Jesus' name great.*

33   Seeing a Rainbow in the Sky – *We can trust and persevere.*

36   Sleeping in a Tent – *Where is your focus? Make the most of your time now.*

39   Eating S'mores – *Let's be thankful that God gives us what we need.*

42   Headlamps & Flashlights – *Fill yourself with his light daily.*

45   On the Shoreline – *Are you saying 'yes' to Jesus?*

48   Skipping Stones – *Jesus should be our strong foundation.*

52   Outdoor Sports – *We are fearfully and wonderfully made!*

55   Nature Scavenger Hunt

57   Daily Drivers

INTRODUCTION

The main goal of *Adventure Box Devotions* is to provide families with children, devotions that can be read together on any outdoor adventure. These devotions are intended to create, build and sustain lasting relationships with one another and especially with Jesus. This book helps families take the Word of God with them and apply it to campouts or outdoor activities. Families will enjoy the interactions of reading, praying, and responding to promptings in this book. *Adventure Box Devotions* brings scripture to life in a more relatable and applicable way that will engage all members of the family. Whether on the road or in the woods this devotional makes scripture reading fun and interactive.

Each adventure that your family chooses has a corresponding scripture, devotion, sights & sounds, and prayer for parents to read aloud with their child(ren). It presents a new and fresh way of experiencing Jesus while being outdoors. *Adventure Box Devotions* will bring a new perspective to the reader: that Jesus is near to us even when we are outside and away from Church, while seeing biblical truths in a more tangible and applicable way to our current locations.

This devotion takes outdoor activities or simple things we do on campouts back into alignment with the Word of God and into Jesus' presence. When we stop, look, and listen to the sights that surround us, we are reminded of the awe-inspiring beauty of God's creation and how near he is to us. While driving on the road or sitting around a campfire, we can spend time with our loved ones and the most beloved of them all, Jesus. He desires to have a real, raw, and unrelenting relationship with us. I hope this book brings you closer to Jesus as you see and experience the beauty of his creation.

HOW TO USE THIS DEVOTIONAL

In the Table of Contents you will find various adventures listed. Determine the adventure you are on or want to take as a family (example: "Streams" or "Stargazing"). Once you have found your adventure, turn to the corresponding page of the book. Parent(s), you will read aloud the scripture and devotion to your child(ren), have them complete the sights & sounds, then discuss responses out loud together. Once you have finished, conclude the devotion by reading the prayer aloud to your family. You will repeat this process for every adventure you take. Be sure to have a pen or pencil for your child(ren) to use in order to respond when prompted in this book.

There is a section delegated for when you are on the road with your family called Daily Drivers. Parents, on these pages you will see several scripture passages that can be read aloud or to yourself before you start traveling on the road. It is a simple way to get some of God's word in your mind before you set out for your adventure. All scripture is referenced from the New Living Translation (NLT).

At the back of the book there is a special Nature Scavenger Hunt for kids to do just for fun! This can be completed as a family or with a sibling. I hope you and your family find these adventure devotions fun, engaging, and inspiring. May you go and grow with Jesus and with one another! Blessings.

GRAB YOUR GEAR

You would never want to leave home without these items when preparing for a hike: a full water bottle, a first aid kit, and a map. For those of you who like to take the extra step of being prepared, adding sun protection and a snack to your bag is always a good choice depending on the type of weather and duration of time you will be hiking. These are just a few essential items we need to go on a safe and successful hike. Leaving behind any of the items could be detrimental. In the same way, spiritually speaking, you wouldn't ever want to travel without these things stored in your heart and mind: your quiet time with Jesus, the Holy Spirit, and memorized scripture verses. Without them, we go unprepared and are vulnerable to challenging situations we might face every day.

Before you set out into the beauty of God's creation, there are a few safety precautions to make note. Depending on where you are headed, make sure to check with the local park office or resource center before going on any trails. There are important tips and rules to follow to for each location. It's always worth the extra trip to go in and get familiar with their maps, safety rules, and regulations before heading out on the trail. Consider these helpful tips if there isn't a local park office or resource center nearby:

1. Never hike alone, always have a buddy system.
2. Stay on the marked trails and don't trailblaze your own path.
3. Follow the rule of "pack it in, pack it out" meaning whatever you bring in your pack should be taken back out with you until you come to a proper disposal area.
4. Don't start any fires.
5. Leave nature the way you found it.

Now, it's time to gear up and get ready as you and your family start your outdoor adventures. Safe travels!

ON A PATH

God helps us make right decisions that lead us to life.

> Jesus told him, 'I am the way, the truth, and the
> life. No one can come to the Father except
> through me.' John 14:6

Devotion: As we navigate through the wilderness we can easily lose our way when we don't have proper essentials such as a map, compass or GPS. When my husband, our children, and I hike on marked trails we sometimes read the map incorrectly and find ourselves on the wrong trail going in the opposite direction of our destination! The same thing can happen to us even spiritually when we are not on the right path.

A path is a way or road that someone else has traveled before you. It takes you from one place to the next. Jesus teaches us that there is only one way to the Father... through Jesus and believing in him. If we follow him, our hearts are on the right path. He is so gracious to us and gives his Holy Spirit who protects, councils, and corrects us. Without his guidance we have a harder time making good decisions which can take us down the wrong path if we aren't careful, like telling a lie to your mom or dad, taking something from a friend without asking, or sneaking a few pieces of candy that your parents have hidden away out of reach. Even worse, it could even be talking back to your parents and speaking disrespectfully. All of these wrong actions can make God's heart sad. Jesus gives us the chance to repent and say, "I am sorry." and ask for forgiveness when we've done something wrong. That's why reading the Bible, staying in community with other believers and praying (which is the way we talk to God) daily is so essential to staying on the right path with Jesus.

I know there are times in my life where I feel like I'm heading in the wrong direction or I feel lost and unsure of what decision I should make. Have you ever felt like you did not know what to do? Or you know what choice you should make and end up doing the opposite? Perhaps you have been tempted to do something wrong instead of doing what was right. We have all been in situations like these, but we can get back on the right path when we ask for Jesus' help and receive his forgiveness. As a result he will tell our hearts the right thing to do and get us back on track.

Those right decisions might be using kind words to your little brother or sister when they frustrate you, doing the dishes when your mom or dad asks you the first time, paying attention and doing your best in school, using your manners around other people, or standing up for someone who might be getting made fun of. All of these little right choices can help you learn to love others as yourself. When we choose to make good decisions with the small stuff, we will be better prepared to make good decisions with the bigger choices in life. If you ask Jesus what the next right thing is to do, he will show you and encourage your heart. So choose what is right because Jesus is the path that we want to follow.

Sights & Sounds: Write an example of a good decision you can make right now to follow Jesus. What can you do to show others how to follow Jesus?

Prayer: Jesus, we are so grateful for your sacrifice and for giving us your Spirit that leads and teaches us your ways of truth and righteousness. Help us to make good decisions by listening to you. For we know that you will lead us to paths of righteousness when we seek you with all our heart, amen.

BY A STREAM

We need to set aside time to rest with Jesus.

> The Lord is my shepherd; I have all that I need.
> He lets me rest in green meadows; he leads me
> beside peaceful streams. Psalm 23:1–2

Devotion: Some of the most peaceful places are found outside in God's creation. Don't you think? There is something so relaxing about being near water. Listening to the gentle trickle or steady flow of water is refreshing to the soul. We each are responsible to take care of our minds, wills, and bodies in a way that pleases God. We do this by taking time to rest, listen, and talk to Jesus. Many times we can get distracted by life and things that keep us busy like school, sports, hobbies, and friends too. None of this is bad and in fact he wants all of these things for us in order to grow. We can get so busy that we forget to pray or even read our Bible! Rest that helps us 'unplug' from our daily routines can bring you closer to Jesus.

Did you know that God set aside a day of rest for you to take from school, friends, sports, and hobbies? It's called the 'Sabbath', which starts from Friday at sundown and ends on Saturday at sundown, but many Christians observe Sabbath on Sunday. The Bible tells us about the Sabbath in the Ten Commandments. Deuteronomy 5:12 says, "Observe the Sabbath day by keeping it holy, as the Lord your God has commanded you." We are reminded that this day is set apart for us to be with God. On the Sabbath we get to rest and not work so that way we can pray, listen to Jesus, and enjoy our time with God and our family.

You can pray or talk with God like you do any other day of the week, but on this day you get to enjoy his presence and take a break from your busy week. There are many things that demand our attention. It might be challenging to set those tasks aside or regular habits we do in order to rest our minds and bodies. If you feel like you are not able to 'unplug' ask yourself, "why?" Is it because you are afraid you might miss out on something? Could it be that you find security in constant busyness? Or could it be that you are worried you might get bored not playing with your friends or doing your usual routine? This is understandable and struggles we deal with. I can promise you that there isn't anything more important that needs to be done than just allowing yourself to rest and be in the peace of your home with your family and with your heart and mind on God.

Time with Jesus is *always* time well spent. He knew we would need rest from our busy week which is why he gave us the gift of the Sabbath. When we allow ourselves to rest we are then better equipped mentally, emotionally, physically, and spiritually to take on a new day. One thing that we must be aware of is that we don't necessarily need a stream or body of water to rest by, though ideally, I would prefer it that way every time I wanted to rest! We can rest with Jesus when we pray, read the Bible, and enjoy our family on the Sabbath. What a wonderful gift God gave us!

Sights & Sounds: Write or draw a picture of how your family rests on the Sabbath. What do you feel like after you rest in Jesus? If you haven't yet, what do you think it would be like? Share your thoughts with those around you.

Prayer: Thank you God for giving us such a beautiful earth. You have made the mountaintops, rivers and streams, creatures large and small. We find so much joy and excitement being in your creation. We need refreshing and we know that it is only found as we rest along-side of you, Jesus. Help us to keep your commandments by observing the Sabbath and spend time with you, amen.

SITTING AROUND A CAMPFIRE

Jesus is closer than you think!

> When they got there, they found breakfast waiting for them - fish cooking over a charcoal fire, and some bread. John 21:9

Devotion: As you sit carefully with your family around a campfire what do you feel? Do you feel the warmth of the hot glowing coals warming your toes? Do you hear the snap-crackling of the wood burning? Or the sweet aroma of yummy, gooey s'mores over an open fire? Mmmmm, delicious! What about the fun conversations your family has around a campfire? There are so many wonderful things we can feel and experience together just sitting around a campfire. The disciples got to live in close proximity to Jesus, eating, conversing, sharing deep emotions, thoughts and struggles with him. Did you know that Jesus also cares about your feelings, your thoughts, your frustrations, and wants to share your excitement and sadness? It's true! Jesus isn't only in a Church building. He is with us wherever we go; even on a campout! When we look back in scripture a lot of the stories that we recount are when Jesus was out traveling from town to town. He wasn't just in a building teaching... he was one-on-one with the people and even in their homes doing life together.

You might be curious how Jesus goes places with us today. When you asked Jesus into your heart he sent his Holy Spirit to live inside your heart and go with you everywhere! At certain times we feel that gentle nudging or burning inside our hearts if we aren't doing what is right and can sense a peace when we are singing praises and spending time with him. He lovingly corrects us through his Spirit no matter where we might be.

Did you know Jesus feels just as much as you do and he wants you to come to him and share your heart with him anytime, anywhere, for all your life? Imagine him sitting with you right now at the campfire. What do you think he would say to you? Do you feel loved and appreciated by him? Or do you feel afraid that you did something wrong and he might be mad? Those thoughts that you might have don't actually reflect his heart on how he feels about you. You are a joy to his heart because you are his precious child in whom he delights. He does not stay angry or upset with us when we do something wrong. He understands and knows that we need his help. Jesus is always near and ready to help you and give you his hand. All you have to do is reach for his.

Sit quietly and let him speak to your heart. Jesus lets us know what is on his mind too. It's especially comforting to know that he is with us everywhere we go and never leaves our side. He is closer than you think, anticipates conversations, and earnestly desires to hear what is on your mind. Jesus doesn't demand anything from us. He wants our hearts to be in a relationship with him more than anything. Look for him in your surroundings, like in sunsets, his beautiful creation, people, in prayer, encouraging words from a friend, the Bible, and even animals! This is how he wants to do life with you: holding your hand, being active and present in your daily life walking out failures and victories! How close are you letting Jesus be in your life?

Sights & Sounds: Write or draw a picture of how you feel sitting around the campfire right now. How close to Jesus do you feel right now? Tell him what is on your heart... he is always listening.

Prayer: Jesus, today in society we often times think you are far away and distant, but this is not true. Our desire is to see you and experience you every day. You reveal yourself to us everywhere we go and not just while we are at Church. May we learn to listen to your Holy Spirit as we invite you into our daily lives. Thank you, Jesus, that you are patient with us and are so willing to draw us back to your heart and want to do life with us, amen.

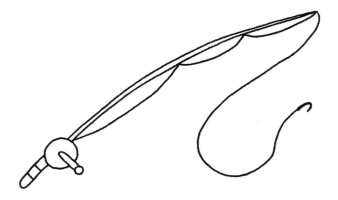

GOIN' FISHIN'

Jesus has something better for us.

One day as Jesus was walking along the shore of
the Sea of Galilee, he saw two brothers - Simon,
also called Peter, and Andrew - throwing a net
into the water, they fished for a living. Jesus called
out to them, 'Come, follow me, and I will show
you how to fish for people!' And they left their
nets at once and followed him. Matthew 4:18–20

Devotion: Peter and Andrew were fishing and received an
invitation from Jesus himself. They weren't just leaving their fishing
nets behind to go follow Jesus. They left their status, their desires
of seeking what they wanted, their money, acceptance from
people, and received a life that was worth living for. Jesus was the
only one who could give Peter and Andrew everything they could
ever need, a life of freedom and salvation. You might be living

your life doing what you want instead of following Jesus' way. He might be asking you to set aside something, maybe upset feelings towards someone, a toy, sport, hobby? Or a friend that might be taking a lot of your time and your attention from work you need to get done? The disciples walked away from a lifestyle that was going to hold them back from a relationship with Jesus. They made the right decision to follow him and in return they were given authority and life with Jesus for all eternity. Ask him what might be distracting you and he will help you to set it aside to seek his heart.

There are times that we have are going to have to put aside or give up something in order to better hear from God. Be encouraged, he is not mad or disappointed. Instead, he wants to help you grow and become the person he created you to be. He has the blueprint of who you are because he made you! It's not that he doesn't want you to have nice things and friends... he does! He has something better to give you if you are willing to give up or let go of something that distracts you from spending time with him. In return we will receive blessings that cannot be taken away.

Just like the disciples gave up their lifestyles to follow Jesus wholeheartedly, we too can give up or let go of things to be less distracted to walk closer with him. God knows that you need things like food, shelter, friends and desires you to become who he made you to be. Jesus has the best plan and path for you to take if you are willing to let go of distractions that keep you from spending time with him and loving him will a whole heart. Will you love Jesus with all your heart today?

Sights & Sounds: Write or draw a picture of what you can set aside in order to spend time with Jesus. Share with someone what it is and ask them to help you stay accountable to any changes you want to make.

Prayer: Beloved Jesus, we pray right now that you will open our eyes to the things that we need to put aside. May our whole heart trust and obey you. For we know that when we seek you with all our heart, we find you and we find out who we are in return. Give us eyes to see, ears to hear and hearts undivided for you, amen.

ON A HIGHWAY (Not while driving of course!)

How can you be a blessing to those around you?

> Listen! It's the voice of someone shouting, 'Clear
> the way through the wilderness for the Lord!
> Make a straight highway through the wasteland
> for our God!' Isaiah 40:3

Devotion: When you want to get somewhere fast a highway is usually the best option. Highways connect smaller cities to larger cities and states. There are many uses for highways and they enable families who live far from one another to be brought close with just a short commute. Many businesses and companies ship goods across land by using highways and supply different cities with food for the people of that area. Highways are very useful, and did you know there were highways back in biblical times? Pretty neat huh?!

The prophet Isaiah heard from the Lord and spoke of the highways that already existed in his time, but also of the ones that were going to be made in the future (which is in our time now!). A prophet is a person who heard from God and was to share with the people the message of God. The reason why God used prophets is because before Jesus was living on the earth God's Holy Spirit was not yet given to people. So in order for ordinary people to hear very important things from God, he would use a prophet to speak to the people. We know that God keeps his word and we can see with our own eyes today that this scripture from the prophet Isaiah has been fulfilled. We should not take for granted our easy access to highways that allow us to travel with ease and speed anywhere in the country. We should be grateful and excited that we can gather together at Church and take adventurous trips with our loved ones.

As God's children, we are to use our abilities and talents to bless those around us by reaching out to other communities to be the hands and feet of Jesus. The prophet Isaiah did this and used his voice to tell those around him about God. You have talents and abilities that Jesus wants you to use for his Kingdom too. His desire is that we go and grow bigger in our cities sharing the good news of Jesus with our communitites. God wants a big Kingdom family and you're part of it!

There are several ways you can help out. You can take food to different food pantries in the city, go visit a sick or hurt person in a hospital, pay for someone's meal ahead of you in the car line, pick up trash in a nearby park, serving food in a soup kitchen, play music on your instrument at a nursing home or even volunteer to work at your school or church. There lots of ways to be a vessel of his light and love. Use your God given abilities to bless those around you near or far. When you drive on the highway again, think of the people around you and how you can make a difference in your community. After all, we have more ways to travel farther because of highways so distance isn't an issue that should keep us from helping others. What can you do to make things better around you? Get creative, get out there, and let your light and love shine bright!

Sights & Sounds: Write or draw a picture of ways that you can serve or help your community around you. Will you travel far or stay close in your community? Map out a plan with your parents to be a helper in your community.

Prayer: Jesus, we are grateful for the improvements of life this day and age. Let us not take for granted the ease and comfort that transportation offers and the chances to grow and be with community. You have given us wisdom to help those around us with your love. May we use our resources to bless those around us as we use the modern highways of your world. We want to make a difference with you and for you, amen.

WALKING AMONG THE WILDFLOWERS

Jesus is the security we need.

> The grass withers and the flowers fade, but the
> word of our God stands forever. Isaiah 40:8

Devotion: The flowers that bloom in the spring fade away and
the leaves that fall from the heights of the trees welcome winter
and become blanketed with snow. From the snowfall of winter to
the hot summer sun we can see our world change all around us.
God is careful to put into motion the changes of seasons; when
they begin and when they end. It's comforting to know that God
established the seasons since the beginning of time, and it hasn't
changed since. When I feel like my environment is changing
and things look messy around me I feel anxious and want to put
things in order. Having a calm and orderly environment makes

me feel secure. I like knowing where things are and for a room to look neat and tidy with everything in its place. Let's be real though, life is messy and more often than not, the space we live in can be messy and unorganized because we are in a constant state of change just as often as the seasons of the year.

When we feel uncertain and our physical spaces feel chaotic we all have tendencies to reach for things that make us feel secure. It's natural to want things orderly and even try to control our surroundings. Our uneasiness is displayed in our reactions to things and we can get bossy, short tempered, frustrated, and lonely. This usually means we are needing security. Has there ever been a time when you felt like your world was upside-down and you felt unsure of your surroundings? In those moments think back, what did you reach for to make you feel more secure? Was it an electronic, a toy, a friend, parents or a sibling? These are all blessings, but they are not necessarily always going to help us when we feel uncertain. If you notice yourself going to one of these for comfort, pause, and reach for your Bible instead. Open it up and start reading some scriptures. Putting the word God in your heart and mind will bring you true security. If you put to memory his words, you will be better prepared next time when you feel anxious.

The Bible never changes because it's God's very own words and we can trust what he says. Inside the Bible you'll find wonderful stories of God's faithfulness to his people, pain and suffering because of sin, but most of all, the redemption and loving faithfulness of Jesus coming to save us and how God used Jesus' life to put order back into the world. Sin and chaos came into the world after Adam and Eve sinned, but thankfully, God sent Jesus to put order back into the world. Sin causes chaos, but the redeeming power of God removes chaos and puts order in its place.

When we look at the intricacies of all living things from the numerous species of flowers, plants, trees, grasses, and animals on earth we see that God gave order to the world. Looking at the detail in just one flower overwhelms me and is a good reminder of how orderly and detailed God really is. He offers us the best security... his love and order. With his love inside of us we can accomplish many things and become better people. He has orchestrated this universe to work as a cohesive unit bearing harmony in all things even when it feels chaotic. Jesus knows that we are constantly changing, and he wants us to continue learning and growing, mentally, emotionally and physically. The good thing is we won't have to do it alone. Though our lives are in constant change and our bodies grow older every day, there is someone that never changes... Jesus.

Sights & Sounds: Draw a picture of the thing that brings you comfort when you feel uneasy. Next, come up with a plan that will help you reach for the Bible instead of your other comfort. Pray together as a family for support, accountability and encouragement.

Prayer: Even when our lives feel unorganized and sometimes chaotic help our minds to recall your word, Jesus. We know that everything won't always be in order or go as we anticipate, but we can trust that you won't ever change or let us down. Thank you for your word and may we continue to memorize it and store it like treasure deep in our hearts, amen.

ENTERING A CAVE

God is with us when we are hurt and afraid.

> There he came to a cave, where he (Elijah) spent
> the night. 1 Kings 19:9

Devotion: Have you ever had pain in your life that you wanted to go away? Maybe someone at school hasn't been nice to you or a friend treated you unfairly? How did you handle the situation? Did you ignore it or tell the person how it made you feel? You have the choice to either confront the problem that is making you hurt or you can live with that pain and think it's okay, but it's not. God doesn't want your heart to hurt and he never wants you to be afraid. There will be times in your life when this is unavoidable. When you feel yourself trying to ignore the problem and turn the other way...stop and take a moment to ask Jesus for help.

Elijah didn't stop to ask for God's help. He ended up running away from his problems for forty days and forty nights and then ended up sleeping in a cave! He was so afraid of the people who were chasing after him that he forgot to ask God for help. Though it might be fun to explore a cave, it's probably not the place we should call "home" and God didn't want Elijah running from his problems, he wanted to help him. A lot of us have done this too. When we encounter a problem, we think we are the only ones who can fix it, when actually God is the best person to talk to about our problems!

Jesus desires you to come to him with all your pains, frustrations and upsets so he can give you the right perspective. That's really reassuring right? He can give you the wisdom or help you need to resolve the problem. With prayer and good counsel, it will in time, change for the better. He is more than capable and willing to take your pains on himself, so you don't have to carry them alone. He has the best plan for you and the best way to heal your hurt and pain if you just ask him to. Remember, that you have a loving family you can pray with to help you in situations also. God gave us our families and we can count on each other for love and support when we need it.

Most of all, when you encounter a problem that you don't know how to solve, pause and take a moment and pray. Invite Jesus into your situation and tell him what is on your mind. Elijah was too focused on the people who wanted to hurt him instead of remembering God's power that would save him. It took him sleeping in a cave to hear God's voice and when he heard it, he knew just what to do. Don't worry though, if you don't hear a voice inside your heart right away. You might all of a sudden have a calming feeling wash over you or have an idea fall into your mind of how to fix things. These are a few ways Jesus answers our prayers when we ask for help. It's not always an audible voice that we hear like Elijah did, so don't be disappointed thinking that's the only way to hear him speak. The best thing you could ever do is get into the practice of making him your first stop. This way, when you encounter a really big issue you already recognize how Jesus speaks to you. With the help of Jesus and your family you will be equipted to resolve the problem. Be encouraged dear friend, you are not alone!

Sights & Sounds: Write or draw a picture of how you felt when a problem wouldn't go away. What did you do to resolve the problem? What will you do differently next time?

Prayer: Jesus, when we encounter problems and pain that seem too big for us to face, remind us to bring them to you right away. We want your help and counsel for we know that you always have the best way to heal our hearts. We trust you Jesus and thank you for knowing us so well, amen.

STARGAZING

You have special abilities to make Jesus' name great.

> He counts the stars and calls them all by name.
> Psalm 147:4

Devotion: Look up at the night sky. What do you see? Stars, right? Lots of them! Did you know that God named each one of them? There are so many stars and immeasurably more than meets the eye. How perplexing the thought that there are so many stars and yet the Lord knows them each by name! My mind can't even fathom the idea. It's beautifully true and when I am out in his creation the more amazed I am by the wonders of God's universe. I hope you realize that since he named the stars which are abundant, how much more he knows you and cares for you! The Creator of the universe has a plan and purpose for your life. You are a delight to him, and just the thought of you brings a smile to his face. Just like he has purpose for the stars and the moon to light up the night sky, he has put purpose within you to be a light that shines bright for him.

We weren't made to do whatever we want, whenever we want. Instead, we are supposed to be willing vessels that use our talents and skills that God gave us to help, bless, and point others to Jesus. You might be really good at playing a sport, an instrument, perhaps an artist that paints pretty pictures or maybe a great student. Whatever your skills are, you can use them to help other people. Get creative with different ways you can express your talents and God given abilities and use them wisely. Teach a friend how to score a goal, paint beautiful pictures and send them to someone just for fun or to someone who is sick.

Write a song and ask to play it for the elderly at a retirement home or during praise and worship at your church. You can even help a friend with their homework and be sure to encourage those around you with kind words. There are numerous ways you can help out as a child. You don't have to be an adult to help someone!

The stars he created have purpose to light up the night sky and tell of the wonders of the Glory of God. Since those stars up above were made to shine, let's be just as bright as they are. So, the next time you pray, ask Jesus what purpose and skills you have that can bless others? You will find it very surprising when he shows you or speaks to your heart. Jesus speaks through his word (the Bible), through people, through nature, worship, and so many more ways because he cannot be contained. He has limitless ways to get your attention if you are listening. You were made to shine brighter than a star and to help make a difference in his world. When you feel small or insignificant just remember this truth: he has called you by name and you are his, just as he has numbered the stars and calls them by name.

Sights & Sounds: Write or draw a picture of your special talents or skills that you want to use to bless others with. Share them with your family as you sit underneath the starry sky.

Prayer: Maker of heaven and earth, we give you glory for your marvelous deeds and the works of your mighty hands. Thank you for creating the earth, the sky above us and for our lives here on earth. Thank you for putting purpose in each one of us. Help us make a difference in your world. May we use the talents and abilities you have given to each one of us to achieve great things with you, we love you Jesus, amen.

SEEING A RAINBOW IN THE SKY

We can trust God and persevere.

> When I see the rainbow in the clouds, I will
> remember the eternal covenant between God
> and every living creature on earth. Genesis 9:16

Devotion: Red, orange, yellow, green, blue, and purple, these are the colors of God's rainbow! After it rains we all know that rainbows form in the sky above. The beautiful colors that glisten in the dewy mist reveal God's steadfast love and promise to his creation. It's not just light bouncing off of water droplets and that's it... although it's pretty neat how science discovered how light refracts and the physical representation that occurs because of this. God's rainbow is a promise that was first revealed to Noah and his family and has remained thousands of years later to

remind us that God always keeps his promises.
A covenant is a promise that won't ever be broken.

A promise is like a bond of trust between two people. The first one, who made the promise to uphold it, and the second, to believe that what they said will happen. Has there ever been a time when someone broke a promise to you? I bet that made you feel sad and upset and made it hard for you to trust that person again, right? Our bonds of trust between one another will be broken at times because no one is perfect, and we all make mistakes. Trusting in God is different though. He is someone that is perfect and can always be trusted. This makes our trust in him feel secure, which then encourages us to keep working hard and persevering in life.

Noah believed what God said would happen even before the rains came. It took him 120 years to build the ark as he committed his life to trusting God that he would eventually send the rain. Can you imagine having to work for that long towards a goal? Talk about commitment! He didn't give up and he persevered through all the hard work not to mention all the teasing he received from people around him through the years as he worked hard building the ark.

Working under pressure and sticking to your goal even when people don't support you or believe you can, is hard. We can feel like our efforts are pointless and we feel like giving up. Has there been a time when someone has teased you because of what you believe in? Or maybe you said something that other people don't agree with? Perhaps, you have prayed asking Jesus for something, and your prayer has yet to be answered. In those moments it's easy to want to quit and stop trusting God. Jesus doesn't promise us a life of ease and perfection, rather we will go through testing and trials that will put pressure on us. That pressure and various hardships will shape our character into who he wants us to be. The difference is, that when we trust and walk with Jesus he always helps us through it. We won't have to be alone to figure it all out. Noah could have ignored God and done things his own way, but instead he trusted and worked hard through the tough times and was rewarded with life because of it. Noah and his whole family survived along with the animals they took with them. When you want to quit, commit your mind to keep trusting in God and persevering towards what you know is right. The next time you pray and think God won't answer your prayers or it feels like your waiting forever for fulfillment of a prayer, remember that God will keep his promises to you even if it takes several years! He is ready to help and wants you to trust in him just like Noah did.

Sights & Sounds: Write or draw a picture of the rainbow you see and how it makes you feel. What other promises or covenants of God come to your mind? Make a list and share them with your family.

Prayer: God, we are grateful that you create, and science discovers your creations and the physical beauties of this world. Thank you for your rainbow in the sky that helps to remind us of your faithfulness. We know that we can trust you with the big things and the little things because you love us, amen.

SLEEPING IN A TENT

Where is your focus? Make the most of your time now.

> For we know that when this earthly tent we live in is taken down (that is, when we die and leave this earthly body), we will have a house in heaven, an eternal body made for us by God himself and not by human hands. 2 Corinthians 5:1

Devotion: Tents are temporary shelters to rest in and take from one location to the next with ease and mobility. They allow for temporary residing in beautiful surroundings that normally wouldn't be accessible. Tents are made of fabric that can be easily torn, flooded, blown down or ripped apart by different elements. These wonderful inventions are not meant to be permanent, but I am certainly grateful for the ease and comfort it provides when we are outside in nature. Wouldn't you say that one of the most exciting things about camping is sleeping in a tent?! It's so fun being under the stars and listening to different animals and critters around you at night. The sights and smells of God's glorious creation surround you can be experienced firsthand with little effort. If something is temporary it means that eventually it will fall apart or deteriorate. We need to view our life here on earth as temporary.

This 'tent' is not my only home. Meaning, the temporal things of this life and what I have right now will not always be with me, but my soul will live forever. What is a soul exactly? A soul is made up of your mind, will, and body. This is what makes you... you! Your thoughts, dreams and desires are all unique and God gave them to you. It's not material things or belongings, rather, it's people's souls that last forever! Too often we hear people say "YOLO", meaning "You Only Live Once." when it's actually more like, "YOLT", meaning "You Only Live Twice." because we have an eternity that waits for us on the other side of this life. Wouldn't you say that people are more important and matter more than clothing, toys, success and money? Who we become matters most in this life.

To make sure we are making the most of our life we should be loving God with all our heart, mind, soul and strength and loving others as ourselves. To achieve this, we need to spend time talking to God, reading the Bible and staying accountable to one another. Our thoughts, words and character need to be shaped now here on this earth and Jesus is just the person who can help you achieve this. Look around you, the world is huge! There are so many people, cultures and nations that God loves so much. Most of all, those people that are around you are people that Jesus loves and wants you to be a light that shines bright for all to see. He wants you to go explore the world and tell others about his love and forgiveness.

Jesus wants you to live out loud looking different and sounding different than people who don't follow him. It's not *just* about doing good deeds, it's about *who you are* and *who you become*. It's about the core motives of your heart. Who are you? What are your thoughts about people? What are your thoughts about God? What do your actions look like towards others? You are responsible for your own soul, which is your mind, will and body. How are you going to cultivate it here on earth is what matters the most.

Time is of the essence and we don't want to waste any of it. It's not about what we own, what we look like, but how we act and whom we become. These motives tell us what our hearts are really full of. So, when you hear someone say, "You only have one life so live it the way you want to!" Remember, that you're here for a reason and you need to cultivate your time here on earth doing what is right. What you do and who you are has an impact on your eternal destiny. Jesus will hold all of us accountable for our lives here on earth, so let's make this temporary life a life that shares the hope and love of Jesus with others. We keep our souls in check as we walk hand in hand with Jesus to our eternal destiny.

Sights & Sounds: Take a moment and write down some ideas of how you can make the environment around you for others, a place to know and experience the love of Jesus. What are some ways to keep your soul (your mind, will and body) in check?

Prayer: Jesus, we have been given the gift of life. We want to do our best keeping our souls in tune with your Holy Spirit. This world is temporary, but our souls live forever. Help us keep our eyes focused on our relationship with you Jesus and to be wise with our decisions of how we live, amen.

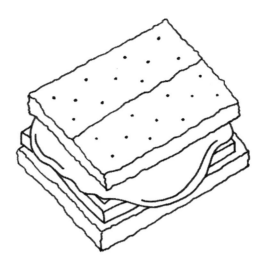

EATING S'MORES

Let's be thankful that God gives us what we need.

> Taste and see that the Lord is good. Oh, the joys
> of those who take refuge in him! Psalm 34:8

Devotion: Mmmmmm, gooey chocolate, warm marshmallows, crunchy graham crackers all in one savory bite! I don't know about you, but when I eat s'mores I end up wanting a whole lot more than just one. I know that one should be enough, so I try to stop there. Do you ever feel like you want more? More toys, games or sweet treats? I think we all have wanted more of something. We are all guilty of wanting more 'wants' instead of being grateful for what we already have.

Have you ever experienced a time when you didn't have a place to sleep? Have you ever gone without food for a few days? Have you ever looked in your closet and not found any clothing to wear? I know these questions might seem silly to ask, but they show us something more. The majority of the time we don't lack any of these things. Sure we might not always have the latest clothing style in our wardrobe, or perhaps we might have skipped a meal here and there because our parents might not have gone to the store yet or we might have even been outside for several hours, but always come home to a place of shelter. A lot of times we can even confuse what wants and needs actually are.

Having the right perspective on what a 'need' is versus a 'want' is very important. Often times we think a need is a new toy, a new bike or a new video game. When actually, those are just wants. It's okay to want those things at times, but when we look at the bigger picture and the perspective Jesus desires us to have, is that he has always given us all that we actually need to live. Real needs are water, food, clothing, and shelter. What's even better is that Jesus is gracious gives us both! Look at all that you own and think about what your real needs are versus your wants. Wants are everything else! It might be a game, a new stuffed animal or new shoes. Have you noticed that you actually have both your needs and wants met? That is something worth thanking God for! He is so generous to give your parents jobs and income to support your family with shelter, food, and clothing.

Unfortunately, there are people out there who do lack these needs and that's when we, as believers in Jesus, get to step up and help our communities with those in need. We can supply them with the things they lack. We are so blessed to have all of our real needs met. I am so grateful that the God of the universe has always given me and my family what we need in order to live and help those around us too! Remember, give thanks to God for giving you and your family all that you need. When you see someone who doesn't have food, clothing or shelter, be sure to let your parents know and ask them how you can help those people who are in need. The next time you have a s'mores take some time to think of all the sweet and good things God has given to you. Thank him for your family and the good gifts he gives. He is more than willing to give you good things.

Sights & Sounds: Write or draw a picture of what good things you have tasted or seen on your trip so far. What can you give thanks to Jesus for today? Share your thoughts with those around you.

Prayer: Jesus, we come to you with our hearts open and full of gratitude. We know that you provide for us and sustain us with good things. May our hearts not forget where these come from... you. Help us to remember what a real need is versus a want and help us to keep a good perspective. Thank you for how faithful and good you really are. We love you Jesus, amen.

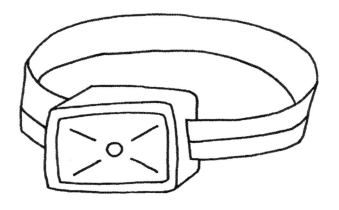

HEADLAMPS & FLASHLIGHTS

Fill yourself with his light daily.

> Your word is a lamp to guide my feet and a light
> for my path. Psalm 119: 105

Devotion: Headlamps. Who knew a small light on an elastic band would become essential for surviving in the woods? I am most certainly grateful for this wonderful and creative invention. I stumble and lose my way and can't see traversing through the thick woods, let alone shuffling through my backpack in my tent without one of these! Light helps us see where we are and where we need to go. Without light we can't see as well. Headlamps and flashlights help us accomplish tasks with ease, safety and assurance. The same is true for our souls. We can't see much or understand a lot that's going on or how to take the next step in our journey with Jesus if we aren't reading the Bible and spending time praying and listening to God. Fueling our soul and spirit with the light of his word is essential if we want to see the path he has put before us. The Bible teaches us what to do and what not to do, how to treat and serve others, it gives many of examples of people's lives and how their mistakes were overshadowed by God's grace, mercy, and forgiveness. God always gives us good direction especially when we ask for his help.

When we read the Bible and memorize his words we are taking in God's light into our hearts. The peace and love that comes from spending time in his word fills us with knowledge of who God is. When we learn more about him we find out what he likes and what he doesn't like. How we can learn from other people's mistakes and make sure we don't fall into the same sin. We can also then pour that knowledge of God and good choices into those around us to better love and serve others. If we aren't using the light (the Bible) to light up our path (our journey in life) we will stumble and fall and possibly turn to the wrong direction away from where God is and is leading us to. I wouldn't want to take the wrong trail when hiking and I certainly don't want to go on a path that isn't safe. Would you?

Has there been a time in your life when you knew the right thing to do and you ignored that small voice inside your heart? Did you ever feel that burning sensation in your chest when you did something or said something you shouldn't have and knew it? Or perhaps you felt that nudge inside of you when you told a lie? That's how Jesus' Holy Spirit leads us and lovingly corrects us. When you might be going in the wrong direction or choosing to do what's bad, he will cause you to feel uncomfortable in your mind and heart to help you turn from it, to repent (to say that you are sorry) and ask for forgiveness. He's not watching you like a judge waiting for you to make a mistake. Not at all! He will gently steer you back to his heart so that you stay protected from harmful things.

Spending time with Jesus is like light to your path so you know where to go and what to do! His Holy Spirit guides your heart to know right from wrong, good from bad and will always help you on your journey if you are willing to listen and obey. I hope that you start your day by filling your heart with scripture from the Bible and your quiet time with Jesus. Your path will be lit up with the presence of God to lead you on your way dear friend.

Sights & Sounds: Write down one scripture verse you have memorized by heart and share it with your family. If you haven't yet, commit to memorizing this memory verse to store his word in your heart: Psalm 119:105 "Your word is a lamp to guide my feet and a light for my path." Read it out loud and recite it to your family.

Prayer: God, we are so grateful for the light and truth of your word. Help us to be mindful and stay in your word feeding our soul and spirit daily. May we cling to it and find rest for our mind and heart. May your Holy Spirit lead us with onto paths of righteousness (right choices) now and forever, amen.

ON THE SHORELINE

Are you saying 'yes' to Jesus?

> Once again Jesus began teaching by the
> lakeshore. A very large crowd soon gathered
> around him, so he got into a boat. Then he sat
> in the boat while all the people remained on
> the shore. Mark 4:1

Devotion: There is something so beautiful about waves crashing
on the shoreline and the sound of water seeping down into the
sand. Those incredible sounds can make us feel calm and more
relaxed, don't you think? I love beaches and lakes! I like to feel
the warm sunshine on my face and sand between my toes. I
especially enjoy the moments when I find a really pretty shell or
rock that catches my eye almost like little sparkling treasures.
There is so much more life beyond the shoreline that lies beneath
the water that we can't see if we just stand on the shoreline.

Think of all the fish, sea creatures, algae, rocks and sand that lie just below the water. It's a whole different world below the water. Which makes me ponder on Jesus' experience when he was teaching to the crowds of people from the boat. They were receiving from him truth that would help them on their journey almost like treasure for their hearts, but they didn't actually get into the boat with him. A lot of them might have taken the words he spoke to heart, but never really changed their lifestyle. They listened from afar instead. I believe there were also people whose lives changed that instant they heard him speak and turned from their life of sin. Do you think there were people so desperate to get close to Jesus that they got in the water? I think so, and there might have been some people who wanted to get in the boat with him too. Especially, the people who had a change of heart and wanted to live a life with Jesus. Let's take that concept and apply it to our own relationship with Jesus.

Jesus desperately wants to take you out on the boat with him. So often we just remain on the 'shoreline' of our heart looking out to Jesus instead of 'getting into the boat' and going deeper with him. Going deeper into relationship with Jesus might look a bit different up close when you are listening to him and seeking him with all your heart. There will be times he wants you to give up something, to forgive someone who has been mean or hurtful to you, there will be times when he wants you to stand strong and speak up to a friend or relative. There might even be a time when you are in pain and feel far from Jesus, but we too are called to suffer with Jesus. He promises to get you through each struggle and pain that you might experience. It's your choice to say "here I am, Jesus. I want to follow you." Your will might not want to, and stubbornness might want to take the front seat of your emotions, but you can put aside those feelings and choose to do what is right. Doing the right thing doesn't always make you feel good in that moment and it might make you a bit frustrated. That's okay, because he understands and we get to work through our frustrations with him. God's will and desire is that you say "yes" to Jesus and get into the boat with him. He will be by your side guiding you with his love and assurance through it all and won't ever force you.

He is willing to teach us if we are willing to say "yes" and listen. He is on the boat and we are on the shore... is he calling you to dive in? Where are you at today in your journey with Jesus? He invites you to go deeper now, just as you are. There is no better time than the present. We can follow our own desires and plans to stay on the shoreline of our heart, but we are only deceiving ourselves. Are you at the shoreline ready to dive into a deeper and more meaningful relaionship with Jesus? Are you willing to say "yes" to Jesus? Going deeper always leads unto more life.

Sights & Sounds: Write or draw a picture of where your heart is today. Is it on the shoreline? Or is it on the boat with Jesus? What changes can you make to go deeper with Jesus? Write them out and share them with your family or parents.

Prayer: Beloved Jesus, thank you for your gentleness and patience as you wait for those to come to you with willingness and open hearts. Our "yes" is what you desire most, and I pray that we will all have a heart that says, "yes" to you so we can grow deeper in our relationships with you. This is the most important thing we can do by cultivating a right heart posture with you. May we lean into you and your ways of life rather than our own, amen.

SKIPPING STONES

Jesus should be our strong foundation.

> The Lord is my rock, my fortress, and my savior;
> my God is my rock, in whom I find protection. He
> is my shield, the power that saves me, and my
> place of safety. Psalm 18:2

Devotion: Have you ever built a house out of blocks and noticed that you can't make it stand up without a proper foundation? Could it stand up for a long time without you holding onto it? Maybe for a little bit, but not long enough right? Sturdy foundations are crucial when making a house out of blocks. Did you know that our hearts also need a strong foundation? Though our hearts aren't a physical house, they still hold something very special... Jesus's Holy Spirit. We have read in the Bible that Jesus is the 'Rock' of Ages and the solid 'Rock' upon which we stand upon and put our trust in. Many people don't have this strong foundation and build their life upon things that end up breaking, falling apart, failing them or even hurting them. Too often, people think that they can get by in life without a relationship with Jesus and good advice from others. They make their own decisions and end up only hurting themselves and those around them because of what they say and do, or how they behave. We all sin and we all make mistakes when we decide that our way is better than God's way.

In order to build a strong foundation you need to make Jesus your number one priority. This means putting Jesus first before your own desires and invite him into the decisions you make. You can achieve this by getting to know him and finding out how he speaks to you. Over time you are then able to trust what he says to be helpful and true. That way, when it's time for you to make a big decision, like if you should forgive someone who hurt you or said something mean to you, you are ready to talk to him about it and then forgive that person. You will be better prepared and have better responses to people and situations you encounter when you have Jesus part of your decision making. When trials come your way, you have a firm rock-solid foundation you can stand upon.

What do you do when you encounter a problem? Do you run to Jesus or run to your friends? Do you ignore your parents when they tell you something that is helpful? This is usually a good barometer for us to use to see if we are trusting in other things other than Jesus. Trusting in yourself is like building a house on a foundation that's made of sand. It might last for a short while, but as the waves (like difficulties and tests) pound away at the foundation, it will all wash away. Having a good foundation in Jesus enables us to withstand all sorts of different trials and challenges.

Imagine for a moment, that you had a good piece of advice from your parents, but you decided to ignore them. You knew deep inside your heart that what they were saying was true and helpful but you didn't want to listen. It's hard sometimes taking good advice that is given to us. Jesus will protect you and has the answer or solution to anything you encounter. He won't make decisions for you though. Your action from this point is either a "yes," I will trust what you are saying or a "no," I will not trust what you are saying and I'm going to do it my way without taking good advice.

Friend, my earnest hope is that you will trust in Jesus and make him your number one priority as you talk to him and seek him first if you are encountering a problem or situation that needs to be resolved. He never wants you to feel like you are alone or can't make a decision, rather he has given you a family that loves you, wisdom that you have stored in your heart, and a free will to make good decisions. With all of these at your side, you can ask Jesus to lead you to the right decision. Your family is a great resource for the big things in your life, so make sure you invite your parents into those places and situations and receive the good advice they have. Let's build a strong foundation of wisdom with Jesus as we invite those who love us to share our troubles and challenging situations.

Sights & Sounds: Write or draw a picture of what kind of foundation you think you have in Jesus right now. Is it sturdy and do you feel like it can withstand the test of time? Or are there areas in which you can build a better foundation with him? Ask him for wisdom and guidance on these matters.

Prayer: There is much purpose in the process of building a foundation with you. Jesus, you are the strong foundation in which we want to build our life upon. Thank you for being the ultimate builder of our souls. You take thoughtful measure to the seasons you have prepared in advance for us; seasons of growing, pruning and refining in order to build a strong and sturdy relationship with you. Continue this good work in us and may we have a heart that is willing to receive wise instruction, amen.

OUTDOOR SPORTS

We are fearfully and wonderfully made.

Thank you for making me so wonderfully complex! Your workmanship is marvelous - how well I know it. Psalm 139:14

Devotion: You are a wonder! From your thoughts to your smile to your hearts deepest desire, God made you for a reason and for a purpose. There is only one you and he wants you to be the very best version of yourself! He delights in seeing you laugh, learn, play and grow. There is nothing more exciting that brings a smile to his face than the thought of you. Do you believe this? Because it's true! He wants you to enjoy life to its fullest measure and even all the fun activities from snowboarding, rock climbing, canoeing, hiking to bicycling and so much more!

Our bodies are super important. Did you know that your body is a temple for Jesus' Holy Spirit to live in?! That sounds really intense... and it should because we are awesomely made in God's image. What's more important is to know and understand how to treat our bodies respectfully and mindfully. Being a good caretaker of your 'temple' (your body) means that you manage your health by eating good food that gives your body energy, getting the right amount of sleep at night, and getting physical activity for our muscles and bones to grow and stay strong.

Imagine for a moment that you want to hike up a mountain and you had donuts for breakfast. You and your family start hiking up the mountain, but you begin to feel tired and worn down. So you grab out of your backpack some candy and eat a few pieces. Do you think that the sugar you had for breakfast and as a snack is going to get you up that mountain? Not very easily, unfortunately. What we put into our bodies matters a lot and did you know that God cares about that too?! It's fine to have some sweet treats here and there and enjoy them, but to fuel our bodies with too much of it and it can cause health problems. Eating a variety of healthy foods like whole grains, vegetables, protein and good fats will sustain your body longer to be able to do the sports and activities with long lasting energy. Jesus gave us these bodies and we want to do our best to take care of them so we can enjoy hiking up mountains, skiing, snowboarding, paddle boarding, ice skating and so much more!

When we choose to treat our bodies in unhealthy ways, we are not taking good care of our 'temple' which God gave us to care for. He wants you to have a healthy body and mind that can perform tasks and learn new things. Not only do we bless our bodies when we do this it is also a blessing to those around us. When we are thoughtful to take care of ourselves, we then do a better job of helping someone else out when we need to perform a physical task with ease and agility. Your job is to do your best by taking care of your 'temple' so you can do great things with Jesus! Will you let him lead you to a better version of yourself that is mentally healthy and physically strong?

Sights & Sounds: Write or draw a picture of how you want to grow physically and spiritually with Jesus. Write out your plan to achieve this goal then share it with your family or loved ones.

Prayer: Jesus, you bless our bodies to perform and function in marvelous ways. Please give us wisdom how to take care of our physical bodies that will be pleasing to you since we (our bodies) are the temple that holds your Holy Spirit. Keep us motivated to choose a healthy lifestyle so we can be helpful to those around us. Lead us with your wisdom to do great things with you, amen.

NATURE SCAVENGER HUNT

Look around in nature to see how many of these things you can find:

ant hill

bird's nest

spider

bee

rock

berries

butterfly

leaf

lady bug

log

ant

pine cone

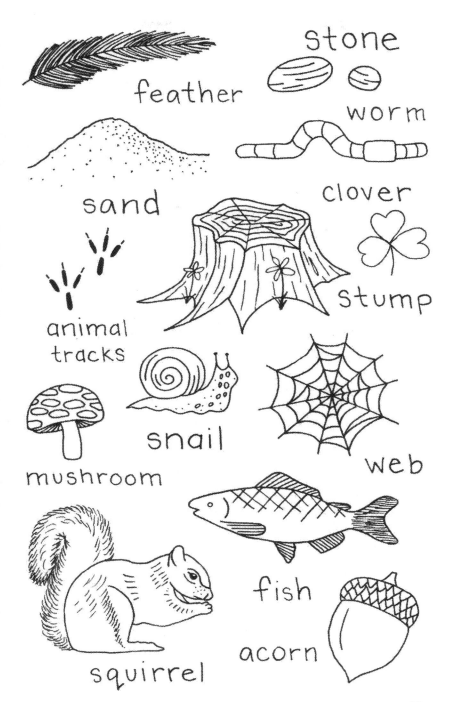

feather

stone

worm

sand

clover

stump

animal
tracks

snail

web

mushroom

fish

acorn

squirrel

DAILY DRIVERS

"DAILY DRIVERS" are to be read before going out on your travels and either read to yourself or aloud with your family in the car. This is a great way for you or the whole family to hear God's word even if it is for a brief moment. We know that even though you may not have time to participate in reading a full devotion before traveling on the road, these scriptures will help keep your mind and heart on Jesus. May you be encouraged by these scriptures and reflect, meditate, and recall his promises to you through his word.

Nehemiah 9:6 "You alone are the Lord. You made the skies and the heavens and all the stars. You made the earth and the seas and everything in them. You preserve them all, and the angels of heaven worship you."

PRAYER: There is no one else like you Lord. We are so grateful for who you are and all that you have made. Your world is beautiful! Help us to take care of it by loving others well and being more mindful of what the earth needs. You were so kind to us to give us dominion over it. May you help us to do what is right for your world and most importantly, for one another, amen.

Psalm 147:4 "He counts the stars and calls them all by name."

PRAYER: You see each one of us. You know us all. You call each one of us by name just as you call the stars by name. How awesome your thoughts are towards us. We want to thank you for being so near and present. Teach our hearts to listen to your voice and to still our thoughts before you. Your name is great among the heavens and among the nations. There is no one else like you Lord, amen.

Psalm 104:1-3 "Let all that I am praise the Lord. O Lord my God, how great you are! You are robed with honor and majesty. You are dressed in a robe of light. You stretch out the starry curtain of the heavens; you lay out the rafters of your home in the rain clouds. You make the clouds your chariot; you ride upon the wings of the wind."

PRAYER: Wonderful creator! You deserve all glory and splendor. None can be compared to you. May our lips bless you and our tongues praise your wonderful deeds. You have made yourself known in your world. May we do our part to be arrows pointing to you and stand out like lights among the darkness. Let us make your name great among all the nations, amen.

Psalm 37:23-24 "The Lord directs the steps of the godly. He delights in every detail of their lives. Though they stumble, they will never fall, for the Lord holds them by the hand."

PRAYER: I am relieved to hear these pleasant promises. That you delight in us and keep our feet from slipping, but only when we seek you. Jesus, you are faithful to put us on paths that lead to prosperity. Only with you do we have life, only when we hold your hand are we kept safe. Thank you Lord, for your promises to keep us all of our days even into eternity. We love you Jesus, amen.

Job 5: 10 "He gives rain for the earth and water for the fields."

PRAYER: Our minds cannot fathom your ways of how you provide for your creation. We are stricken with awe by your creation. You take care of this world and everything in it and you most certainly take care of me. Thank you for knowing me and giving me all that I need, amen.

Matthew 6:25-27 "That is why I tell you not to worry about everyday life- whether you have enough food and drink, or enough clothes to wear. Isn't life more than food, and your body more than clothing? Look at the birds. They don't plant or harvest or store food in barns, for your heavenly Father feeds them. And aren't you far more valuable to him than they are? Can all your worries add a single moment to your life?"

PRAYER: Beloved Savior, you hold all things together. You are always aware of all that we need. We lack no good thing from your hand for you sustain us with good things. Our hearts and minds tend to wander away from you and worry about the stress of life when our eyes are not fixated on you. In those moments may your sweet Spirit lead us back to you and trust that you have the next right thing for us, amen.

Isaiah 55:10-11 "The rain and snow come down from the heavens and stay on the ground to water the earth. They cause the grain to grow, producing seed for the farmer and bread for the hungry. It is the same with my word. I send it out, and it always produces fruit. It will accomplish all I want it to, and it will prosper everywhere I send it."

PRAYER: We are grateful Lord to know that all your promises are truth and we are watching your Spirit move upon this earth. All your covenants and promises still stands and will continue to come to fruition because of your faithfulness. May our lips speak the truth of your word in our own lives and those around us to be influencers and a people who make a difference because of your Spirit. Thank you that you want to include us in the process that we may see the fulfillment of scripture in our days until you come back for us Jesus, amen.

Habakkuk 2:14 "For as the waters fill the sea, the earth will be filled with an awareness of the glory of the Lord."

PRAYER: More and more people know of you and have given their lives to you Jesus because of what your disciples did long ago. Your fame has been spread across the nations to those near and far. May we continue to share with those the hope of Jesus so we can see your promises fulfilled and the glory of the Lord fill the earth as the waters fill the sea, amen.

Proverbs 3:13-15 "Joyful is the person who finds wisdom, the one who gains understanding. For wisdom is more profitable than silver, and her wages are better than gold. Wisdom is more precious than rubies; nothing you desire can compare with her."

PRAYER: When we seek you God, we find wisdom. For you give it freely to those who seek you and desire you. May our hearts not long for the things of this world, instead, may we incline our hearts and ears to your voice and receive from you the knowledge and wisdom we need to live a godly life, amen.

Daniel 12:3 "Those who are wise will shine as bright as the sky, and those who lead many to righteousness will shine like the stars forever."

PRAYER: Lord, make our hearts diligent in the work we put our hands to. May we accomplish great things for your kingdom and not for our own selfish gain. Let our works be unto the fame of your name among the nations... to make your name great. Help us make the next right decision that will lead to greater life with you, amen.

Psalm 119:105-106 "Your word is a lamp to guide my feet and a light for my path. I've promised it once, and I'll promise it again: I will obey your righteous regulations."

PRAYER: Jesus, our desire is to be diligent with our time management so we can be with you every day. We want to be in your word, in prayer, and relationship with you. May your words fill our hearts and minds as we meditate on them day and night so we will obey your commandments, amen.

Hebrews 11:1 "Faith is the confidence that what we hope for will actually happen; it gives us assurance about things we cannot see."

PRAYER: Desire stirs our hearts to make a difference and in you Jesus, we have a hope that cannot be shaken. Strengthen our souls to keep perspective while we go about our days. Remind us that even when we don't see our prayers answered right away, dreams or desires fulfilled that we can still hope for what you have promised long ago, an eternity with you Jesus, amen.

Psalm 124: 8 "Our help is from the Lord, who made heaven and earth."

PRAYER: There is no other source of strength or power that can help us. You alone Lord Jesus are our ever-present help in times of trouble. Looking to anything else will not suffice and provide for us the help we need. We don't just seek your hands Jesus to help us, we also seek your face and desire a real relationship with you. We want you as our number one priority, amen.

Psalm 19:1-2 "The heavens proclaim the glory of God. The skies display his craftsmanship. Day after day they continue to speak; night after night they make him known."

PRAYER: You speak Jesus and from eternity past to eternity present, you are God. You alone establish the earth and everything in it. We bless you Father for making this vast universe. Your ways are magnificent and far beyond what our feeble minds can fathom. Thank you God for your awesome power that by your spoken words, life is birthed and sustained. You are forever Holy God, amen.

Ecclesiastes 3:11 "Yet God has made everything beautiful for its own time. He has planted eternity in the human heart, but even so, people cannot see the whole scope of God's work from beginning to end."

PRAYER: Lord, make each day count and enable us to be okay with the process of time. We spend so much of our days worrying about situations and circumstances that don't matter. Let us not lack diligence in pursuing what we should. Help us to be mindful of the time and how precious it is and that we cannot jump into another season until you take us there. Thank you that you know what we need when we need it, amen.

Matthew 6:28- 30 "And why worry about your clothing? Look at the lilies of the field and how they grow. They don't work or make their clothing, yet Solomon in all his glory was not dressed as beautifully as they are. And if God cares so wonderfully for wildflowers that are here today and thrown into the fire tomorrow, he will certainly care for you. Why do you have so little faith?"

PRAYER: Big and little, you see it all Lord. You see all the thoughts and worries that can consume our minds. You are careful to meet each of us where we are in life even if we have a lot or little on our minds. Stressors can distract us from spending quality time with you and rob us of intimacy. Teach us to let go of the petty things that distract us from you and your presence. May our hearts learn to take captive over false narratives, and may we live knowing that you care for even the smallest details of our lives. We love you Jesus, amen.

---

2 Corinthians 5:7 "For we live by believing and not by seeing."

PRAYER: Jesus, you keep all life in motion. You determine our days and have given us all that we need to live a life of godliness. Though we cannot see your face physically, we feel and know your presence spiritually. You are not far from us...teach us to know that the physical life we experience and see is just a glimmer of the truth life we will have with you in eternity. Give us the right perspective to remember that the spiritual life is even more real than what we experience in the physical, amen.

---

2 Corinthians 5:17 "This means that anyone who belongs to Christ has become a new person. The old life is gone; a new life has begun."

PRAYER: When you enter our souls we no longer desired to do what our old nature wants. We see the contrast of light and dark immediately and shun from evil to pursue righteousness. We don't want our old nature and sinful ways to creep back in. Rather, we desire to walk in your ways hand in hand with you Jesus. Please help us live a righteous life following in your footsteps, amen.

Proverbs 16:9 "We can make our plans, but the Lord determines our steps."

PRAYER: Lord, our days are filled with goals, dreams, and desires. All which you have put inside our hearts. We know that you are the one who leads us to our destination. Help us to remember it is not in our own will power that we make these things come to fruition, rather by your grace and guidance and in your perfect timing these are fulfilled. Thank you Jesus, for giving us each a special gift and may we remember to cultivate it and may it be used to make your name great, amen.

Jeremiah 10:12-13 "But God made the earth by his power, and he preserves it by his wisdom. With his own understanding he stretched out the heavens. When he speaks in the thunder, the heavens roar with rain. He causes the clouds to rise over the earth. He sends the lightning with the rain and releases the wind from his storehouse."

PRAYER: Who can stand against you? None can withhold you from your mighty power God. You have established the earth and provide for all living creators. Nothing is too difficult for you. May your wisdom lead your people, and may we have eyes to see, ears to hear, and hearts to understand your ways so that we will not fall into sin against you. Lead each of us on our path that ultimately leads to you, amen.

2 Timothy 3:16-17 "All scripture is inspired by God and is useful to teach us what is true and to make us realize what is wrong in our lives. It corrects us when we are wrong and teaches us to do what is right. God uses it to prepare and equip his people to do every good work."

PRAYER: Your words were established for a purpose. The very words were set in place for a reason. It wasn't by accident that you chose the prophets and people inspired by your Holy Spirit to write and teach us. Your words have accomplished and will continue to accomplish your purpose. We need your correction, discernment and guidance. Without these, we fall short and miss the mark. Thank you that you are sovereign, and you teach us, correct us, and equip us to do your will, amen.

Psalm 23 "The Lord is my shepherd; I have all that I need. He lets me rest in green meadows; he leads me beside peaceful streams. He renews my strength. He guides me along right paths, bringing honor to his name. Even when I walk through the darkest valley, I will not be afraid, for you are close beside me. Your rod and your staff protect and comfort me. You prepare a feast for me in the presence of my enemies. You honor me by anointing my head with oil. My cup overflows with blessings. Surely your goodness and unfailing love will pursue me all the days of my life, and I will live in the house of the Lord forever."

PRAYER: Jesus, you are all that we could ever need. May our number one desire be a heart that yearns for you and seek you as our number one priority. Let our feet follow in your footsteps and may we have an insatiable desire to read your word, giving you a heart that is un-divided all of our days, amen.

Printed in the United States
by Baker & Taylor Publisher Services